Discover Through CRAFT

WEATHER AND SEASONS

By Jillian Powell

W
FRANKLIN WATTS
LONDON • SYDNEY

First published in 2014 by Franklin Watts
Franklin Watts
338 Euston Road
London NW1 3BH

Franklin Watts Australia
Level 17/207 Kent Street
Sydney, NSW 2000

Series editor: Amy Stephenson
Series designer: Jeni Child
Crafts: Rita Storey
Craft photography: Tudor Photography
Picture researcher: Diana Morris

Picture credits:
AlaskaStock/Alamy: 20t. Guido Amrein Switzerland Shutterstock:
26-27bg, 31t. Andia/Photoshot: 24tr. Galyana Andrusko/
Shutterstock: 14-15 bg. Blueskystudio/Shutterstock: 6-7bg.
Ronald Caswell/Shutterstock: 22-23 bg. Clover Photoshot: 16tr
Creative Travel Projects/Shutterstock: 1. Digoarpi Shutterstock:
4bl. Ehp73/istockphoto: 18t. Lane V Erikson/Shutterstock:
4br. J P Forte/istockphoto: 11t David R Frazier/Alamy: 11b.
Robert Harding PL/Alamy: 15t. Irink/Shutterstock: 16tl. Joruba/
Dreamstime: 23b. Joyfull Shutterstock: 16c. KarimKamon/
Shutterstock: 32b. Katrina 1/front cover tr. Kemeo/Shutterstock:
8cl. Alan Kiehr Alamy: 27t. Lucyna Koch/istockphoto: 20b.
nicky-m/istockphoto: 16tc. Mallivan/istockphoto: 15b. Andrew
Mayovskyy/Shutterstock: 7b. Aliaksander Mazurkevich/
Dreamstime: 8cr Vasiliy Merkushev/Shutterstock: 14b. Mikkolem/
Dreamstime:5t Dan Mirica/Shutterstock: 16bl. Olga Mittsova/
Shutterstock:18-19bg. Zoltan Mucsi Shutterstock: front cover c.
Marvin Nauman/UPPA/Photoshot: 26b. Nadav Neuhaus/WpN/
Photoshot: 18b. Alexandra Nika/Shutterstock: 23t. Noppharat/
Shutterstock: 10c. Paul Orr/Shutterstock: 10-11 bg. Bill Perry/
Shutterstock: 12t. photographerlondon/Dreamstime: 19t.
Radoiu/Dreamstime: 30 Redeyed/Dreamstime: 22b Michael
Schmeling/Dreamstime: 7t. Mark Sisson/FLPA: 8r. Solarseven/
Shutterstock: 27b. Stanny/Shutterstock: 16cr. Stockelements/
Shutterstock: 12b. Swa182/Shutterstock: 28t thehague/
istockphoto: 5c. Tinors/istockphoto: 22t. Lily Trott/Shutterstock:
8l. Nickolay Vinokurov/Shutterstock: 24cl. wikipedia: 6b.

Every attempt has been made to clear
copyright. Should there be any inadvertent
omission please apply to the publisher for
rectification.

Dewey number: 508.2

HB ISBN: 978 1 4451 3098 9
Library ebook ISBN: 978 1 4451 3585 4

Printed in China

Franklin Watts is a division of Hachette
Children's Books, an Hachette UK company.
www.hachette.co.uk

CONTENTS

Words in **bold** can be found in the glossary on page 30.

Some of the projects in this book require scissors, paint, glue, baby oil, a glue gun and a pin. We would recommend that children are supervised by a responsible adult when using these things.

WHAT CAUSES WEATHER?

We experience weather all of the time, but what makes it change from day to day?

The weather is always changing

Weather is caused by changes in the state of the Earth's **atmosphere**. This is the layer of gases that surround the Earth and make up the air we breathe. These changes mean the weather can be hot, cold, wet, dry, windy or calm. Lots of other things help make weather, such as the air temperature, the speed of the wind and the direction it is blowing in and whether there is bright sunshine or a cloudy sky.

Weather vanes point in the direction the wind is blowing. This French vane is pointing west. (Ouest is the French word for west.)

Cold and wet weather can produce snowstorms or blizzards.

Symbols on this weather map tell us what the weather is like in different places around the world.

Weather maps

Weather **forecasters** use maps of a country or a place to tell us what the weather will be like there. They use symbols to show where it will be sunny or cloudy and where it might rain or snow. They can also show us information such as temperature, wind speed and direction and how the weather might change.

When areas of warm and cold air meet they form warm or cold weather **fronts**. Warm air is lighter than cool air because it is less **dense**. When warm air rises, cool air will take its place below. This movement of warm and cold air creates changes in the weather.

Weather and us

Weather can affect lots of things, such as the clothes we wear and the outdoor activities or sports we do. It is important for farmers as they need the right amount of sun and rain for their crops to grow and produce a good harvest. The weather can also affect travel. Cars, lorries, trains, ships and planes can be affected by bad weather, such as strong winds, fog, snow or heavy rain that causes flooding.

People enjoying the sunshine and hot weather on a beach.

Quick FACTS

- The weather is caused by changes in the Earth's atmosphere.
- It is always changing.
- It affects us and the things around us.

WEATHER AND SEASONS

The tilt of the Earth's axis as it travels around the Sun gives us our seasons.

All change

Just as the weather can change each day, it also changes with the seasons. The Earth takes one year to **orbit** the Sun. The Earth's **axis** is tilted at an angle so when one half (or **hemisphere**) of Earth is pointing towards the Sun, the other half is pointing away. The hemisphere that is pointing towards the Sun is in summer, the other hemisphere is in winter. The Earth also spins on its axis, which creates day and night. It takes 24 hours to complete each spin.

Spring
(Autumn)

Summer
(Winter)

Winter
(Summer)

Autumn
(Spring)

This shows the seasons for the Northern Hemisphere. The seasons for the Southern Hemisphere are shown in brackets.

The seasons

In **tropical** regions, between the **equator** and the Tropic of Cancer or the Tropic of Capricorn, it stays warm all year. There are only two seasons, a wet and a dry season. In **temperate** regions, which lie between the tropics and the **polar circles**, there are four seasons. As Earth orbits the Sun, the hemisphere in summer gradually begins to tilt away from the Sun and its season changes from summer into autumn. As the other hemisphere begins to tilt towards the Sun, its season also changes, from winter into spring.

Polar Circle (Arctic)

Tropic of Cancer

Equator

Tropic of Capricorn

Polar Circle (Antarctic)

The four seasons

In spring, the Sun begins to climb higher in the sky and it is daylight for longer. There is more sunshine and the air gets warmer. Summer is the warmest season because the Sun is at its highest in the sky. Summer has the most daylight hours, with long evenings.

In autumn, daytime gets shorter and the Sun begins to get lower in the sky. Less daytime means less Sun, so the air begins to get cooler. Cooler temperatures and damp air can make it misty or foggy in the mornings and evenings. As winter arrives, the Sun is at its lowest in the sky. There are fewer daylight hours, so the ground has less time to warm up. The temperature drops so it feels cold.

The Sun is much lower in the sky in the winter. Less daylight means it is colder.

QUIZ TIME!

In which direction does Earth spin on its axis?

a. clockwise
b. anticlockwise
c. both

Answer on page 32.

? How do the seasons affect animals and plants? Turn the page to find out.

Spring to summer

As the seasons change they affect living things around us. In spring, with more hours of daylight and warmer temperatures, trees and plants begin to grow. Buds open into flowers that bees and other insects will **pollinate**. Spring is also the time when many baby animals are born. Some birds and animals **migrate** with the seasons. Swifts and swallows fly from Africa to Europe for the summer, to find food and to breed.

Autumn leaves

In autumn, trees and plants begin to prepare for winter. **Evergreen** trees stay green all year but the leaves on **deciduous** trees and plants change colour. The trees stop sending water to their leaves so the leaves begin to dry out and lose their green colour. They turn red or yellow and then fall off the tree.

Lambs are usually born in the spring.

Baby swallows in their nest in the summertime.

Leaves turn red and yellow in the autumn.

A dormouse hibernating in a nest in the winter.

Winter hibernation

In winter, icy and snowy weather can make it hard for animals to find food and stay warm. Some animals hibernate, which means they find a warm and dry place and go into a deep sleep. They won't wake up again until the spring.

QUIZ TIME!

The colours found in natural things, such as leaves, are called:

a. pigtails
b. pigments
c. pigstyes

Answer on page 32.

Make this

Autumn leaves come in lots of beautiful colours. Make a seasonal wreath from fallen leaves to go on a door, or for an autumn display.

You could make a wreath for every season. What kinds of things could you find to put on a winter, a spring or a summer wreath?

1 Carefully cut out a large ring from cardboard, or cut the centre out of a paper plate.

2 Glue on lots of autumn leaves. Keep overlapping them until the whole ring is covered.

3 Glue on acorns, berries and pine cones. Leave to dry.

4 Loop a piece of ribbon through the wreath. Hang it up.

SUNSHINE AND TEMPERATURE

The Sun warms the temperature of the air.

❄ The Sun's energy

Every living thing on Earth needs the Sun's warmth and energy. The Sun is very hot – its surface is about 5,500 degrees Celsius. The huge distance that sunlight has to travel through space to reach Earth and the Earth's atmosphere help to protect us from this fierce heat. The heat from the Sun warms up everything, including the air around us.

The Sun's energy warms up the Earth's land, water and air.

! WARNING: Never look directly at the Sun. It is so bright it can damage your eyes.

A thermometer showing that it is a warm day. The temperature is 25°C.

Measuring temperatures

Weather map symbols show the Sun with a number. This is the temperature in degrees Celsius (°C) measured on a **thermometer**. When the air temperature rises, the liquid in a thermometer **expands** and moves up the scale. When it cools down again, the liquid **contracts** and moves back down the scale. When the temperature rises to 30°C, it feels hot. At around 15°C, it feels mild, and at 5°C it is cold. If the temperature falls to 0°C, it is freezing.

Daily temperatures

The season and the position of the Sun in the sky both affect how warm the weather feels. As the Sun rises in the sky it begins to warm up the ground. Heat from the ground rises, which also helps to warm up the air temperature. The air is warmest in the early afternoon, when the Sun is high in the sky. At night, when there is no sunlight, it feels colder. The coldest time is usually just before sunrise.

Quick FACTS

• The air temperature changes with the seasons and the time of day.
• We often measure temperature in degrees Celsius (°C).

? What else do you think affects the air temperature? Turn the page to find out.

Mountains, valleys and deserts

The air temperature is cooler in high places. On mountains, it drops by around 6.5°C for every 1,000 metres you climb. The air here feels cooler because it is often windy in high places. The air higher up is also thinner than air lower down and cannot hold the heat that rises from the ground. The hottest places on Earth are some **deserts** and low-lying dry valleys, such as Death Valley in California, where the temperature

Death Valley, in California, USA, is one of the lowest and hottest places on Earth.

can reach over 57°C. The coldest place on Earth is in Antarctica, which is also the world's biggest desert. Temperatures here stay below freezing all year round and can fall to around minus 89°C.

A hot and sunny day in Central Park, New York, USA.

Towns and cities

In towns and cities, the air temperature is usually warmer than in the country. This is because buildings store heat from the Sun during the day. As the air cools at night, the buildings release the stored heat into the air, warming up the temperature.

Cool shade

Clouds, trees, buildings and sun umbrellas can all block out the Sun and give shade. Even on a hot day it feels cooler in the shade, because we are not feeling the heat from the Sun's rays directly upon us.

HAVE A GO
Take a thermometer out on a sunny day and try taking readings in the sunshine and in the shade at different times of day. Make a bar chart to record your readings at set times.

Make this

The Sun's rays are blocked and reflected by this suncatcher. Notice what happens when you put it in bright sunlight and in a breezy spot.

You could experiment with different colours. Which colours produce the best effects?

1 Ask an adult to cut off the top section of a large plastic drinks bottle. Paste torn pieces of tissue paper all over it with glue. Leave to dry

2 Tape a piece of cling wrap to a table. Paste 3 or 4 layers of torn tissue paper all over it using watered-down white glue. Leave to dry.

3 Peel the tissue paper layer off the cling wrap. Using a jar lid to draw around, cut out lots of circles from the tissue paper layer.

4 Cut four lengths of string. Tape circles along each string. Tape the strings to the bottle top. Hang up your suncatcher near a window using more string.

RAINY WEATHER

Rain is part of the Earth's water cycle and all living things need water.

All plants, animals and people, need water to live. The water cycle is the way the Earth's water is constantly recycled. As the Sun heats the water in rivers, lakes and oceans, water droplets **evaporate** and turn into **water vapour**. This vapour rises into the air and cools. As it cools, the water vapour **condenses**, turning back into tiny water droplets. The water droplets gather together to form clouds and as the droplets are blown about and bump into each other they get bigger. The clouds get bigger as the drops get larger and heavier, until the clouds can't hold any more and release them as rain.

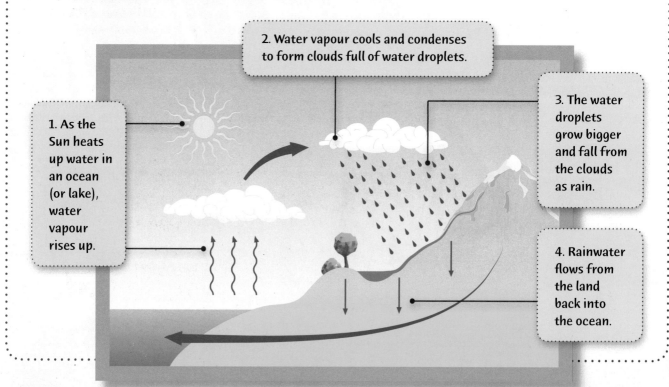

2. Water vapour cools and condenses to form clouds full of water droplets.

1. As the Sun heats up water in an ocean (or lake), water vapour rises up.

3. The water droplets grow bigger and fall from the clouds as rain.

4. Rainwater flows from the land back into the ocean.

Quick FACTS

• All living things need water. • The Earth has only so much water, which it constantly recycles through the water cycle.

Rainfall

Rain that falls onto the land forms puddles. Some rain soaks into the ground and is taken up by the roots of plants. Some goes even deeper into rocks in the ground. Water that falls into rivers and streams flows back into lakes and oceans.

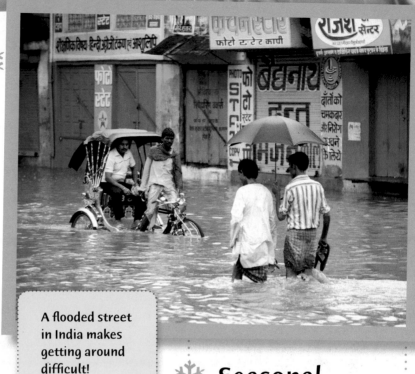

A flooded street in India makes getting around difficult!

Rain and us

We need rain because we all need water to drink. Farmers need rain for their crops and animals. Some places get more rain than others. Hilly and mountainous areas usually have more rain than low-lying, flat areas. This is because as air rises over mountains, it cools down. The water vapour condenses, falling as rain or snow. Heavy rain can sometimes cause flooding, but if a place has no rainfall for a long time, land and rivers can dry up and cause a **drought.** Deserts can go for months or even years without rain.

A drought has caused a river bed to dry out and the earth to crack.

Seasonal rains

Some parts of the world, including parts of Africa, Asia, Australia, South America and North America, have heavy seasonal or **monsoon** rains that arrive after weeks of hot dry weather. They arrive when winds that are blowing from the land, change direction to carry moist air from the ocean onto the land.

? How do clouds tell us whether it is going to be rainy or fine weather? Turn the page to find out.

Clouds

Clouds can tell us what kind of weather to expect. We can learn to spot rain clouds and tell then apart from fine weather clouds. Small, white and puffy clouds (1) or high wispy clouds (2) mean fine weather. Huge, puffy white clouds (3) can mean a short spell of heavy rain and dark, dense clouds (4) can bring storms. Flat grey clouds (5) mean drizzle or light rain.

1. Cumulus

2. Cirrus

3. Cumulonimbus

4. Nimbostratus

5. Stratus

The different coloured bands in a rainbow over a village in Mexico.

Rainbows

If the Sun shines when it is raining we may see a rainbow. Sunlight looks white but it is actually made up of different colours. As the Sun's rays shine through a raindrop, the different coloured light rays bend and separate so we see all the colours that make up sunlight as a rainbow.

HAVE A GO

Cut the top section off a clear plastic bottle, take the cap off, turn it upside down and push it back inside the bottom of the bottle. Draw lines on the bottle, marking 1 cm sections, starting at the bottom. Place the bottle outside to catch the rain (you may need to push it into the ground a little so it doesn't fall over). Record the daily amounts on a bar chart. Remember to empty the bottle each day.

QUIZ TIME!

How many colours can you see in a rainbow?

a. 5
b. 7
c. more than 100

Answer on page 32.

Make this

The **Aztec** people thought that using a rainstick could bring on a rainstorm. Your own rainstick will make the sound of falling rain – perhaps you'll even make it rain!

1

Draw around the end of a cardboard tube onto a piece of white card. Repeat to make a second circle.

2

Cut out the two circles, but cut 1 cm larger than the line you have drawn. Make lots of tabs by snipping from the edge to the line.

3

Tape one of the circles to one end of the tube. Use the tabs to overlap the end of the tube. Make sure it is stuck down tightly.

4

Scrunch some newspaper squares into balls. Add these and a handful of rice into the tube. Tape the other card circle tightly to the open end of the tube.

5

Cut a piece of coloured paper to fit around your tube. Tape in place and decorate with paint, string and feathers.

Tip your rainstick onto one end. The rice moving through the tube should sound like rain!

SNOWY WEATHER

Snow and ice can form when the temperature falls below freezing.

When the temperature falls below 0°C, moisture in clouds can freeze. Sometimes water droplets freeze into sleet as they fall, or become freezing rain, which freezes as it touches the cold ground. If water droplets are carried up by drafts of air inside clouds, when they meet cold air they can turn into hail stones or snowflakes. As more water vapour freezes around them, the frozen droplets become bigger and heavier until they begin to fall as hail or snow.

Polar bears live on the ice in the Arctic. They are adapted to live in cold places.

QUIZ TIME!

What colour is a polar bear's fur?

a. blue

b. white

c. It has no colour

Answer on page 32.

Snowy places

Mountains and other high places, and areas that lie within the polar circles get the most snowfall. In the Arctic and Antarctic, there is snow and ice all year round. The animals that live here are adapted to living in the cold. Polar bears (left) live in the Arctic. They have a thick layer of fat under their skin, thick fur and they even have fur on the bottom of their paws. The **Inuit** people of the Arctic are also used to living with the snow. They use snow sleds, **snowmobiles** and skis to get around.

Snowstorms

Snowstorms can bring heavy snow. If it is also windy the snow can blow into blizzards, making it hard to see. Heavy snow can cause problems for transport and farmers. But snow can also be fun for people who enjoy winter sports, such as sledging, skiing and snowboarding.

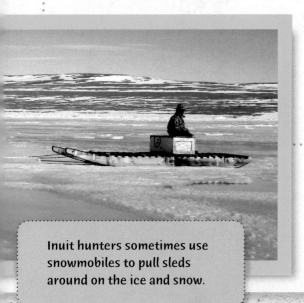

Inuit hunters sometimes use snowmobiles to pull sleds around on the ice and snow.

Quick *FACTS*

• Snow, ice, sleet, hail and frost can all form when the temperature falls below freezing.
• Snow can can be a lot of fun!

? How many sides does a snowflake have? Turn the page to find out.

SNOWIEST PLACES

The top 5 snowiest places in the world are

1. **Mount Rainier, Washington, USA**
2. **Niseko, Japan**
3. **Mount Fidelity, Glacier National Park, Canada**
4. **Alta ski area, Utah, USA**
5. **Alyeska, Alaska, USA**

Lots of tiny ice crystals make up these beautiful snowflakes.

Frost

Frost forms when the air temperature falls below freezing and water vapour in the air freezes into ice crystals on a cold surface, such as plant leaves or a window. When there is enough moisture in the air, it can cause ice crystals to grow and cluster into a **hoar frost**.

The ice crystals in a hoar frost cover the branches of a tree.

Snowflakes

Snowflakes form when moisture in clouds begins to freeze around tiny bits of pollen or dust in the air to form ice crystals. As they begin to fall, more water vapour freezes around them, forming clusters of ice crystals that make snowflakes. Snowflakes have six sides, but each one is different and can be made from up to 200 ice crystals. They look white because of the way light reflects off the crystals.

 HAVE A GO Leave a piece of black paper in the freezer and put it outside when it snows. Use a magnifying glass to examine the snowflakes that fall on it.

Make this

There might not be any real snow in a snow globe, but you can have lots of fun making a wintry scene. You could make one to celebrate Christmas!

When you shake the snow globe you become the wind moving the snow. What happens when you shake it gently? What happens if you shake it a bit harder?

1 Press some plasticine into the bottom of a clean glass jar. Add a plastic figure (or an object such as a tree).

2 Ask an adult to fill the jar with baby oil. Add some glitter. (Make sure you add enough as this will be the 'snow'.)

3 Put on the lid. This must be done up tightly! Ask an adult to help you seal it with some more plasticine or a hot glue gun.

4 The glitter will settle at the bottom of the glass jar. Shake it gently to make the snow begin to swirl.

WINDY WEATHER

Wind is moving air. Warm air rises and cool air sinks; this movement creates the wind.

Warm and cool air

When the Sun shines, the air near the ground gets warmer. Warm air rises because it is lighter and less dense than cool air. Cooler air comes in below it to take its place. This movement of the air creates the wind.

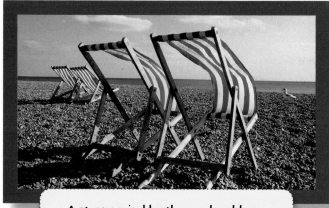

A strong wind by the sea has blown these deck chairs inside out.

Huge waves, caused by windy weather, crash over a lighthouse.

Windy days

We can't see the wind, but we can feel it when it blows in our faces or hair. When we are out on a windy day, it can be hard holding onto hats or umbrellas and we can even find it difficult to walk against a strong wind. We can also see how windy weather affects things around us. It blows through trees and bushes and makes them lose their leaves and even their branches. It can also make lakes and seas rough or choppy, bringing big waves onto the seashore.

A windsock traps the wind, showing its strength and direction.

Measuring winds

Winds are named after the direction they blow from. So a north wind blows from the north and a south wind from the south. Wind socks are used at airports and other places to show how strong the wind is and which direction it is blowing from. The speed of the wind can be measured using an **anemometer.** When it is placed in the wind, the arms on the anemometer spin, showing the wind speed in kilometres per second. Weather forecasters describe wind conditions using the Beaufort wind force scale that measures them from 0–12.

BEAUFORT WIND FORCE SCALE

0=calm
1=light air
2=light breeze
3=gentle breeze
4=moderate breeze
5=fresh breeze
6=strong breeze
7=near gale
8=gale
9=strong gale
10=storm
11=violent storm
12=hurricane

The cups on the arms of this anemometer catch the wind and make it spin.

QUIZ TIME!

When the weather is very windy we sometimes say it is...

a. **breathing a gale**
b. **blowing a gale**
c. **puffing a gale**

Answer on page 32.

? Which places do you think are the most windy? Turn the page to find out.

Windy places

We feel the wind most in open places, such as fields, hilltops and by the sea, where it can blow without anything blocking its way. Buildings, trees and hedges act as wind breaks, and where there are mountains, wind often blows into the valleys that lie between them.

Kite surfers enjoy windy weather at a beach in Wissant, France.

A dust storm in the Sahara desert.

Winds of the world

There are different types of wind around the world. Monsoon winds change direction, blowing from either the oceans or the land to bring wet and dry seasons. The Sirocco is a hot, dusty wind that blows from the Sahara desert. The Mistral is a cold, dry north wind that blows in southern France in the winter or spring.

The wind and us

Strong winds can sometimes cause problems for transport. High bridges and even roads may have to close when winds are dangerously strong. But the wind can also bring people fun when they enjoy outdoor sports like sailing, wind surfing, hang gliding or kite surfing.

Quick FACTS

• Winds are named after the direction from which they blow.
• They are measured from 0–12 on a wind scale called the Beaufort wind force scale.
• Open spaces are often the windiest places.

Make this

The arrow on a weather vane always points in the direction the wind is blowing from. So if it is pointing to the 'S' then there is a southerly wind.

Take your vane outside. Use a compass to make sure the 'N' on the weather vane is pointing to the north. Watch it move when the wind changes direction.

1 Paint the back of a paper plate. When dry, divide it into four sections – N, E, S and W. Weigh it down with a blob of plasticine.

3 Cut a triangle and a tail shape from card. (Make the triangle smaller than the tail shape.) Cut a slot in each end of a straw and push the shapes into the slots.

2 Decorate a paper cup with weather symbols. Glue it onto the plate, over the plasticine. Push a pencil (with a rubber on the end) through the cup and into the plasticine, as shown.

4 Carefully push a pin through the straw and into the rubber on the pencil. It should be able to swivel around freely on top.

TIP: If your weather vane blows over in the wind, weigh it down with more plasticine or hold it down with pebbles.

STORMY WEATHER

Stormy weather can bring floods, strong winds, thunder and lightning.

Floods

When heavy rain falls for a long time, rivers may flood. This means they become so full that they overflow their banks. Flooding can also be caused by high tides and strong winds along coastlines, or when so much rain has fallen that the soil cannot soak up any more water and it can't drain away through underground rocks.

HAVE A GO
Collect some pine cones and place them outside or on a window sill. Watch what happens to the cones when the weather is dry and when it turns wet or stormy.

A city street in the USA is completely flooded after a tropical rainstorm.

Wild winds

Hurricanes and tornadoes are powerful storms with strong, damaging winds. Hurricanes are called typhoons and cyclones in different parts of the world. They form over warm oceans, when strong winds blow together, forcing warm moist air upwards. When they reach land, they bring heavy rain, strong winds and huge waves that can damage buildings, trees and cars.

A hurricane lashes palm trees and a beach in Miami, Florida, USA.

A tornado forms over land when a column of warm moist air rises quickly. As the air rises and mixes with colder air, differences in wind speed and direction can make it rotate or twist. It gets faster and faster as it draws in more warm air. Water droplets in the moist air condense into rain or hail, and if the twisting column of air touches the ground, it becomes a damaging tornado or 'twister' storm.

A tornado or 'twister' touching the ground, destroying the crops in a farmer's field.

Quick FACTS

• When warm air rises very quickly over sea or land and meets cooler air, super storms called hurricanes and tornadoes can form.
• Storms can damage things, such as crops and cause flooding.

? What do you think causes thunder and lightning? Turn the page to find out.

Lightning striking the ground near a city at night.

Thunder and lightning

Thunderstorms happen when warm moist air rises suddenly and quickly, forming dark, puffy clouds that carry on growing and rising. As the warm air meets much cooler air, water vapour inside the clouds turns to water droplets, hail and ice crystals. They bump into each other as they are carried up and down by drafts of air. This bumping creates **charges** of electricity in the clouds and on the ground below them. When these charges connect, they form an electric current and release heat and energy that we see as a flash of lightning.

Lightning flows between clouds or from a cloud to the ground. It heats the air violently, making it expand so quickly that as it cools it explodes with a booming sound, which we hear as thunder. We see lightning before we hear thunder because light travels much faster than sound.

QUIZ TIME!

What is a flash of lightning called?

a. a blizzard

b. a blaze

c. a bolt

Answer on page 32.

Make this

You can make a lightning cracker to create your own thunder! It squashes the air to produce a cracking sound when you flick it downwards.

1
Fold a sheet of A4 paper in half, lengthways. Open it out and lay it flat.

2
Fold each of the four corners in so the points touch the centre line as shown.

3
Fold in half again, along the centre fold. The opening should be facing you.

4
Fold in half again so the points meet. Then open it out again.

5
Fold the two top corners down as shown. It should make a diamond shape.

6
Fold it back on itself so the two points are facing you. Hold the two points and flick the cracker down, hard.

GLOSSARY

anemometer a device for measuring the speed and force of the wind

atmosphere the mixture of gases that surround the Earth

axis an imaginary line through the centre of an object

Aztec the native peoples of Mexico during the 13th to 16th centuries CE

charge in this instance, a store of electrical energy

condenses turns from moisture in the air to liquid

contracts gets smaller

deciduous a type of tree or plant that loses its leaves each year

dense heavy and thick

desert a place with very little or no rainfall and few plants

drought a long period with little or no rain

equator an imaginary line around the centre of the Earth

evergreen a type of tree or plant that keeps its leaves all year

evaporate turn from liquid into gas

expands gets bigger

forecaster in this instance, a person who predicts the weather

front the edge of a moving mass of warm or cold air

hemisphere half of the Earth, either north or south of the equator

hoar frost large clusters of ice crystals that form on plants and other surfaces

Inuit the native peoples of northern Canada, Greenland and Alaska

migrate to change habitat, moving from one region to another

monsoon seasonal winds that change direction, to bring wet or dry seasons

orbit to travel around something

polar circles the Arctic and Antarctic areas, around the north and south poles

pollinate to carry pollen to a plant to fertilise it

snowmobile a small motor vehicle with skis for travelling over snow

symbols objects or pictures that represent something else

temperate belonging to the temperate zones, between the tropics and the polar circles

thermometer instrument that measures temperature

tropical belonging to the tropics, the areas above and below the equator, between the Tropics of Cancer and Capricorn

water vapour moisture in the air

BOOKS

***The Changing Seasons* (series)**
by Paul Humphrey (Franklin Watts , 2012)

Earth Cycles: Seasons by Sally Morgan
(Franklin Watts, 2012)

Project Geography: Weather
by Sally Hewitt (Franklin Watts, 2013)

Popcorn: Science Corner: Weather and Seasons
By Alice Harman (Wayland, 2013)

WEBSITES

www.bbc.co.uk/schools/whatisweather
BBC education website with easy to find information and interactive learning activities on weather

www.metoffice.gov.uk/education/kids
The Met office education site for children, with lots of facts, activities, interactive games and experiments, with a weather explorer guide to help navigate around the site.

www.weatherwizkids.com
A lively American website packed with information on different types of weather, with a useful glossary, interactive games and activities.

NOTE TO PARENTS AND TEACHERS:

Every effort has been made by the Publishers to ensure that these websites are suitable for children, that they are of the highest educational value, and that they contain no inappropriate or offensive material. However, because of the nature of the Internet, it is impossible to guarantee that the contents of these sites will not be altered. We strongly advise that Internet access is supervised by a responsible adult.

INDEX

QUIZ ANSWERS

Page 7. b – anticlockwise

Page 8. b – pigments

Page 16. c – over 100. There are seven main colours in a rainbow (red, orange, yellow, green, blue, indigo and violet), but the human eye can actually see over 100 shades of these colours!

Page 18. c – it has no colour. (Polar bears look white because their fur reflects the colour of the snow.)

Page 24. b – blowing a gale

Page 28. c – a bolt